THE HUMAN

THE WISDOM IN GOD'S DESIGN OF HUMANITY

MYSA ELSHEIKH

The Human: The Wisdom in God's Design of Humanity
Copyright © 2024 by MYSA ELSHEIKH
Published by MUSK STANDARD
www.muskstandard.com
info@muskstandard.com

All rights reserved. No part of this book may be reproduced, translated, or transmitted in any form or by any means, electronic or mechanical, including photocopying, recording, or any information storage and retrieval system, without written permission from the author and/or publisher.

ISBN: 978-1-916800-00-7 (paperback)
ISBN: 978-1-916800-01-4 (e-book)

CONTENTS

Introduction	v
Chapter 1: The External Design	1
Chapter 2: The Internal Design	53
Chapter 3: The Diversity of Human Races	61
About the Author	73

Introduction

This book explores the wisdom behind God's design of humanity. It argues that the human form seems to have a design of inherent purity, implying creation by a pure Creator, who is God. Encouraged by Quranic verses prompting reflection on the self, this book explores various aspects of human anatomy, both internal and external, dissecting their design and the purity they symbolise, thus suggesting divine creation. The fact that there can be taken meanings from the design of humans further supports the notion that an intelligent designer created them, thus refuting the notion of random formation in evolution. In Islam, humans are considered

The Human

highly. Adam, the father of all humans, was created to be a Caliph of God on earth, and the angels prostrated to him following God's command.

Humans can be considered to be formed from four constituents: the body, mind, soul, and ego. The body, akin to animals, is tangible and driven by primal needs. The mind, like the angels, embodies profound intellect and knowledge. The soul encompasses empathy and a sense of otherness, akin to the spiritual beings known as jinn. Lastly, the ego, akin to the desire of trees for sustenance, symbolises human neediness and rootedness in the material world.

There are indeed six races of humans: Africans, Arabs, Indians, Persians, Caucasians, and Asians. Each race is further divided into tribes. In the Quran, God emphasises the creation of people in races and tribes to come to know each other in peace. It is stated that the best people in the sight of God are the most pious. The Prophet Muhammed (peace be upon him), is the greatest worshiper of God and considered the epitome of humanity's spiritual excellence. This correlation between piety and excellence aligns with the concept that the highest knowledge is the knowledge of God.

In Islam, God is considered "Perfect" (Quran 16:60 and 30:27), and the Quran also affirms that God created humans in "a perfect form" (95:4). In the Hadith, Prophet Muhammed (peace be upon him) said, "Adam was created in the image of God." (Bukhari). This means that it is in the design that proclaims the existence of God, as God is not a physical entity in Islam for humans to have His image. The Quran acknowledges humans as signs of God's existence, dedicating two chapters to humanity (one called "the human" and another called "the humans"). This book, in its detailed analysis of the human form, aims to convince the reader to the belief that humans are beautiful creatures created by a pure God.

The human is created in the image of God
their design confirms a truth to be told
Humans came from Adam and Eve from the time of old
they are dignified not to be bought or sold
They are kind, never evil, nor emotionally cold
Jinn and Angels the human form they copy and fraud,
it is time to accept our humanity, people of the world

Chapter One

The External Design

The Human Face

The human face has a pure plan; the nose is long and protruding, like a male penis, and the mouth is empty and internal, like a female vagina. The male and female aspects of the face do not meet or touch and never join, unlike in the genitalia, where they join when the male enters the female during sex. This lack of union of the male and female in the human face emphasises purity and divine creation by God. This resemblance sparked debates among Islamic scholars regarding whether the face should be deemed "*aura*" (shameful) and must be covered. The Quran mentions several times the idea of the face association to worship. In the Quran God says "their sign is in their face from the act of prostration" (48:29) and "establish the human face to purity. It is God's nature that He created in human nature. There is no change to what God creates, that is the upright religion, but the majority of people do not know"(30:30).

Women cover their face in Islam, as their face has no moustache and beard, so no emphasis to purity on face using hair. This lack of extra purity in women's faces mean they were considered shameful to show in public, as perverts may perceive their facial exposure as a desire for sex and may harass or rape them. Prophet Muhammed (pbuh) in one hadith allowed women to uncover their face and hands since the facial design supports the existence of God.

The human stands tall, raising the face high, symbolising their inherent purity and capacity to perceive and worship God, as depicted in Islam. In Christianity, they say God is pure but then contradict it by saying God has a son. Contrastingly, certain Christian and Jewish beliefs attribute human-like attributes or fatigue to God, suggesting imperfection. Islam, on the other hand, portrays Allah as pure and unchanging, resonating with the purity reflected in the human face.

The External Design

The human face is proof that humans can be contacted by God, receive messages from Him, and worship God. In English, the word "faith" is similar to the word "face". In Islam, Muslims worship God in prayer by placing their face on the ground in prostration. Before this, they purify themselves by washing their face, hands, and feet using pure water. The Prophet Muhammed (peace be upon him) said, "Looking at a beautiful face is worship"(Mala Ali Gari). In one hadith, Prophet Muhammed (pbuh) said "seek help from those with beautiful faces"(Asuti). There is also a strong prohibition against hitting people or beating the face. The idea that there is a design of purity in the human face that proves the existence of God means that Muslim women are prohibited from covering their faces during prayer and during pilgrimage in Mecca.

The human face is usually rounded which symbolises purity since a round shape means need. The face separates the male nose and female-looking mouth, so there is a need and no giving. Moreover, the head's cube/ball shape underscores its purity and place of thinking, as the cube has corners that can be felt, while the roundness suggests purity.

God, who is pure, after creating a face with a pure sex plan, gave different parts of the face, such as the nose and mouth, a job to hide the idea of sex in the face further, proclaiming greater purity in humans.

The human face with its pure plan of the separated male nose and female mouth embodies many aspects of human existence:

1. Humans consider purity such as chastity as being important. This is true since many people are offended by foul language, sexual innuendo, and explicitness. The Quran also mentions the early Muslims making vows of chastity; a tradition that still exists in Islamic spirituality such as Sufism (Ihsan), made by dervishes. However, the Islamic vow of chastity allows marriage unlike that of Christian monks and nuns who do not marry at all.

2. The human, as a creation with a pure plan on its face, is evidence that it was created by a pure God, which explains why there is so much spirituality and religion in humans. This also explains why the majority of people believe in a God.

3. The face, counting the pure joining of the male nose and female mouth, an interrupted act of sex, means that sexual desire is intense in humans, and that is natural since sex is the way humans are created and are thus protected from extinction.

The External Design

4. The human face contains shapes similar to genitalia acknowledges humanity's capacity for wrongdoing and repulsiveness.
5. The lack of joining of the male nose and female mouth, means lack of sex, and lack of life, and therefore is understandable that some humans can be infertile and cannot produce children.
6. Some human faces are not pretty to look at, and this reflects the truth of the existence of structures such as the nose and mouth that look like human genitalia, which may be perceived as offensive.
7. The purity of the human face that shows the idea of sex as well as gives a sign of God elevates discussions on sex to a solemn level akin to discussions about God.
8. The purity of the face supports the existence of a pure God, therefore the existence of very beautiful and very handsome people. This is because belief in God is a beautiful thing in the world.
9. The existence of the idea of sex in the human face means people usually find faces to be the most attractive part of the human body.
10. Since the human face has a separated male nose and female mouth, it represents a lack of sex and, consequently, a lack of human beings and life. It

is no surprise humans die and don't live forever in this world. The face is both a symbol of no sex and therefore no life, and is also a sign of the creator, so people knew that once they die, they return to the creator God.

11. Since the face has the joining of the male-looking nose and female-looking mouth, traditionally homosexuality of relations between two males or two females, was seen as being strange and outside the human design, and is the basis for it being considered unnatural and against God.

12. Human design is proof that there is God, thus it is no wonder that in humanity there are prophets, saints and pious humans who have and express great love for God and religion.

Yawn

Shahg in Arabic is when a person is surprised for no reason, so they open and widen their eyes and mouth. Prophet Muhammed (peace be upon him) said yawning is from the devil, as it signifies being astonished at nothing and for no good reason. This is like worshiping or giving reverence to other things other than God. The etymology of "yawn" is probably from "you own," meaning worthy, such as *shahg* from "*shai hag*," meaning the "thing truth/honest." The

Prophet Muhammed (peace be upon him) advise covering our mouths during yawning to avoid the devil.

Sneezing

Sneezing, often following a yawn, expels droplets of saliva, symbolising the spreading of purity, such as belief in God. The Prophet Muhammed (peace be upon him) said he detests yawning and loves sneezing. After sneezing, it is customary for the sneezer to express gratitude , "Thank God," to which others respond with, "Mercy upon you," followed by the sneezer seeking forgiveness for both parties. Modern science says sneezing is healthy, since it's the body's way of ridding from microbes.

Nose

The nose is the long protruding flesh on the human face. Arabs believe the nose is a symbol of self and dignity. In Arabic, the word for the nose is "*anf*," which is similar to the word "reject or annihilate." In English, the word "nose" could be from "no is," emphasising negation. This could be because the greatest knowledge is to be able to say what a thing is not. This idea of rejecting in the nose could be because it exhales air after inhaling it, as if rejecting it. Nevertheless, breathing in and out air is essential for life, more important than food and water to humans. Rejection is the opposite of an agreement to union or joining and, therefore, the purity of the nose. The nose rejects the air, which is nothing, again emphasising that the nose is a protruding flesh opposite the empty mouth.

The nose has two circular holes situated at its lower end. Round shape symbolises need since it is a bent line, while the pair of nostrils signifies duality and emphasises the purity of the nose and face. Therefore, the nose knows of the pure plan of the face, indicating the necessity of intimacy through its dual openings, yet contrastingly, the mouth, with its dividing teeth, represents a departure from this purity. Because the nose looks similar to the penis and male genitalia, and it has the two nostrils that represent the need for sex, men traditionally ask women for sex and marriage.

The nose produces a clear sticky liquid when crying or when one is ill with a cold or flu. The stickiness signifies connection, while the clarity denotes purity. The air going in and out is the opposite, again emphasising genders and their union in the face. Air is clear and difficult to detect, so it is pure, and therefore, it is associated with face in breathing.

Some women pierce the nose, and it is controversial in some cultures such as Arabs. This is because beautifying the nose not only carries meaning of appreciating breathing to life, or enjoyment of perfume, but as the nose looks like a penis, beautifying the nose is seen as expressing love of the penis and sex. Traditionally in Sudan, piercing the nose was done by prostitutes but recently it has become fashionable and more mainstream.

In Arab cultures, where intellect and thought hold prominence, the nose embodies concepts of self and unity. Phrases like *ragmm anfak* (literally against your nose), symbolise coercion or imposition against one's will. In the United Arab Emirates and Gulf, Arab men touch nose to nose in greeting to signify equality, mutual respect and generosity. In Sudan, the expression *alnafss waheda* (lit desire is one) underscores the universality of human desires and the need for mutual respect. Air represents need since it is not detected except if it is moved around, such as by a hand flapping. Therefore, in Arabic, the word for air is *hawa,* which is also used to mean want or love. Therefore nose that breathes air symbolise need, giving and generosity.

Mouth

Mouth in English is possibly from "more is". Since the mouth has a vacant space, it emphasises the absence of joining between nose and mouth, making the face pure. Part of the beard is the hair underneath the lip. It emphasises the emptiness of the mouth, since hair is devoid of feeling.

In embarrassment and shame, girls sometimes cover their mouth and nose with their hand or in danger or shock, since the mouth looks like the genitalia–the place of harm.

Additionally, the mouth has a water-like liquid that is saliva, giving further meanings of the absence of senses and purity. The mouth also has teeth that cut food into smaller parts, further emphasising the division between nose and mouth and its meaning of purity. The fact that humans need to eat food and cut them with their mouths means that purity is essential to human life. Furthermore, the mouth has water, emphasising that it is empty, as water is devoid of sense. This water, called saliva, functions to soften food during chewing and digestion.

Tongue

The mouth has a long muscle called the tongue, which is possible from the words "two on go" to mean the joining which must be done. In Arabic, *Lisaan* derives from "*li saw an*" (what I will do), indicating its role as a muscular organ facilitating connections and actions, thus underscoring its importance. Having a tongue is, therefore, a sign that humans are important creatures, and the tongue itself is important in its use in taste, language, and articulation. The Prophet Muhammed (peace be upon him) said he loved sucking the tongue of his wife, Aisha, signifying help in her important chores.

People spit saliva to distance harm, as saliva is from the mouth, which cuts and so is a place of harm. In Islam, spitting while reciting a prayer is seen as curing illness.

Lips

Lips are smooth flesh and slippery and are not coarse in texture, symbolising purity and freedom from harm. In Arabic, lips are called *shiffa,* which means a cure or lack of harm, as if to hope people do not feel any harm from the cutting of teeth. Teeth are solid and white, meaning the mouth has strong ideas of purity since it shadows the absence between the nose and mouth. As sex involves the genitalia which are a place of harm, people usually kiss the lips as a way of being kind, and wishing safety and smooth sailing as they have sex.

The lips symbolise safety and kindness and restoration, therefore there is the idea that kissing things make them better. This is like a mother kissing the injury on her child to comfort them.

Teeth

Teeth that are slightly separated are seen as beautiful but means harm due to their cutting action, leading to destruction and absence. Therefore, it was seen as a show of kindness and mercy, like the description of Prophet Muhammed's (peace be upon him) teeth in the Hadith. As the Quran states, Prophet Muhammed was sent as a mercy to the world to teach people to worship God so they are not burnt in the hellfire forever.

Smile

A smile is the act of parting the lips and stretching them sideways to reveal teeth, signifying readiness to aid and warn against harm. This is because when people smile they expose their teeth, which cut and therefore are harmful. The term "smile" is possibly derived from "is am ill" or Arabic *ibtisam* from "*ib ati Sam,*" implying a rejection of harm. Thus, humans smile to say they will help people and warn people against harm. Prophet Muhammed (peace be upon him) said smiling is charity, as it shows mercy and kindness between people that are willing to help others.

Sleeping

Sleeping is part of being human. The purity in face and no joining of opposites meaning no touch and no awareness so humans sleep for periods of time, as a form of deprivation from awareness. Prophet Muhammed (pbuh) said sleep is the brother of death. Dreams happen during sleep to indicate that there will be life after death, and that humans have souls and awareness besides that of the body.

Eating

Eating is the process of cutting and dividing food, emphasising the pure face, which divides and separates the male-looking nose from the female-looking mouth. Humans eat, and some even enjoy spicy food emphasising with the pain of cutting. Drinking liquid requires no cutting, so it is kind and usually more enjoyable than solid food, especially for kids and newborns who survive on breast milk. The Arabic word for drink, *sharab*, (*shar ab*) conveys the notion of refusing harm, reflecting kindness and the absence of destruction. The Quran mentions a spicy ginger drink in heaven for the righteous. In Sudan, Arabs give their guests juice to drink as a show of kindness to the guest.

Burping

Burping sound after eating and becoming full from eating has a possibility of symbolising harm. That much cutting of food, means that the person is becoming dangerous, and this is the reason it is disliked by people.

In other words, the sound of burping is an indication that the person is harmful. This self awareness to harm in the person is a sign of purity and goodness in humans.

Forehead

The forehead is an empty part of the face; it lacks creation so it is pure since there is nothing being joined there to create an organ. Traditionally some Arabs preferred higher foreheads, because it distances the hair seen as impure to the rest of face carrying meanings of purity.

Eyes

The eyes are two ball-shaped sensory organs above the nose. If the nose looks like a penis, then the eyes are the testicles. Eyes produce tears, clear liquid-like water that drops down cheeks in sadness, happiness, or even allergy. Eyes sometimes produce a white or yellowish thick liquid in the morning.

Eyes are two, the number of pairs required for sex, which is part of the pure plan of the face. The eyes sense from a distance, unlike taste which requires food to touch the mouth and tongue. Objects can be perceived by the eyes without physical contact. This highlights the purity and distance inherent in visual perception. The round shape of the eyes symbolises desire or need. It reflects their ability to perceive from a distance without touch. The most common eye colour is black or brown, as it is a colour to emphasise the distance by representing absence. Eyes see the outline of objects, the end of objects, or the edge of joining, so it is pure.

Eyes are white to emphasise the need for light since the colour white symbolises the colour of light. White is also the colour for purity, so it further emphasises the meaning of purity in the eyes. Sight in Arabic is *Bassar,* derived from "*be e soor,*" meaning to become aware of the outline. The outline of the eye itself is an elongated round shape, stretched to the sides, a round shape of need and absence; elongated on the side further signifies purity. Additionally, the presence of hair around the eyelids and eyelashes, devoid of feeling, emphasises the eyes' purity.

Moreover, the eyes have hair around the outline of the eyelids and the eyelashes. Since the hair has no feeling, it emphasises the purity of the eyes. Prophet Muhammed (peace be upon him) used Kohl, an eyeliner, to emphasise the outline of the eye to support purity and for women to keep their distance from him to be chaste.

There is a line of hair above the eyes called the eyebrow, which is called *Hajib* in Arabic, meaning veil or barrier. The eyebrows act as a barrier between the pure eyes and the edge of the forehead, where skin meets the hair, and it is impure since it is the meeting of opposites, the unfeeling hair and the skin that feels touch.

In Islam, after visiting God's pure house in Mecca during the pilgrimage, male Muslims are commanded to shave their hair as a sign of purity. The eyes sit above the nose and mouth as an emphasis on elevating purity. In Islam, women are not allowed to shave their eyebrows or make them very thin, as the eyebrows are a sign of purity in the face, and therefore prostitutes used to thin their eyebrows to suggest they are not pure women and offer sex services that are impure.

Additionally, the eyes produce a water-like liquid called tears and, in Arabic, *demoa*. This further emphasises the purity of eyes and face. They are produced in sadness and sometimes even in happiness. Tears drop from the eyes and slide down the cheeks to emphasise the separation between mouth and nose. Therefore, they are called tears from tears or separate and divide. When there is a strong separation between men and women and no life is created, it evokes a sense of sadness. Prophet Muhammed (peace be upon him) said hellfire would not touch a person who cried out of fear to God.

Eyes produce a thick yellow substance—especially in the morning after sleep—called eye booger or rheum. Yellow is a colour that symbolises harm since it lacks the purity of white. For example, fried white onions turn yellow once white becomes absent. The solid thick liquid is joining, so it is impure, so to be yellow is to say joining and impurity is harmful or wrong, so it further emphasises the purity of eyes. In Arabic, it is called *gada*, which means verdict since it states that joining is harmful.

Since the soul and spirit are awareness of other than the self, it is awareness from a distance, and since eyes sense and see from a distance, the eyes are said to be the windows of the soul. Humans close their eye for a great part of the day, during sleep, which is a form of rest from the activities of the day.

Ears

The ears are two to emphasise the genders required to produce life. Also, they detect sound, which is joining or touching between two things. The ears are to the sides to avoid the nose and mouth, where there is a lack of joining meanings. The side is also pure since things on top are in touch, but when side by side, there is little touching, so there is a meaning of purity of ears. So, the ears are designed to hear pure speech and sound, such as the Quran, the speech of the pure God. The ears are a half circle; that is to say the absence of the middle and the middle of humans is where joining or sex happens.

Therefore, the ears, in their shape, carry the meaning of purity.

Ears produce wax, a thick material, and so have ideas of joining. It is like a sound that is produced by hitting or joining two objects. Wax is brown coloured, and brown is a little giving since it is a shade lighter than the black, colour of absence. The brown wax is, to say, little joining; so again, the idea of purity.

People pierce the lower part of the ears to wear jewellery such as earrings in order to beautify the ears and express the importance of the sense of hearing.

Cheeks

The cheeks are the flesh to the side of the nose and mouth. They confirm the idea of the male and female in the face, since in meeting of the male and female is new life or new flesh. Some people have a depression or dent on their cheeks called dimples and it is as if someone is pressing a finger on the cheek. As the cheeks confirm getting from sex, dimples were seen as beautiful and a sign of fertility.

Hair

Hair is a material that has no feeling. It is opposite to skin that feels when touched. This means the joining of the hair to the skin is a meeting of what is different. This meeting of opposites is impure and symbolic of sex, so Muslim women and men cover their hair in public to proclaim purity, chastity, and belief in God. Hair can have dandruff which is a white flake that is oily. Oil is a symbol of identity that slips away and a yellow warning of harm as if telling people off for touching ownership. Hair in humans is on top of the head, which elevates ideas of purity. In animals such as horses, hair on the body suggests they are greedy to senses and degrade lack of touch as animals are creatures of intense physical desires.

Most people in the world have black hair, since the colour black symbolises absence and hair is devoid of feeling or sense. Hair does not feel it represents the spirit and soul, since spirit is about being aware of other people without touch or even for them to be present. Women usually have long hair. This is because hair symbolises absence and the females have absence or emptiness in the genitalia. Men usually have hair all over their bodies, because meeting of the opposite, as hair touches the skin, is a reminder of creating and men usually do more work and think more about sex.

Historical curly hair was seen as beautiful as it emphasises curves and round shape in the body of women such as eyes, breast, waist and bum. Curly hair also emphasises spiritual being, such as communicating with people and going back and forth, understanding people, and awareness outside of self.

Traditionally, people supported certain hair styles which have meanings, for instance splitting hair to half and half, is to say choices and sanity. Or side split to say some are more, some are less, can make ethical decisions and are kind. Since hair on the head carries sexual meanings, being bald is seen as being a man who lacks sexual thinking, that's why it's associated with old age. However, in Islam, men shave their hair as a form of purity, such as after pilgrimage, and it is said that Prophet Muhammed's (pbuh) companion, cousin and son-in-law, Ali ibn Abi Talaib (raa) was bold for he was a pure and religious man.

In old age hair turns grey and this is a sign of purity since old people are less interested in sex, and become more worshiping of God.

Moustache

A moustache is the hair between a male nose and a female mouth, separating them further, suggesting purity. In Arabic, it is called *shareb* derived from *shar ab* (refuse harm), since women are separated from men for safety. Therefore, stronger men do not harm them. The word "moustache" is possibly from the words "most-ache," meaning great harm in risks of women being with men.

Beard

The beard is the hair on the lower jaw; its meaning is to purify the joining of the lower and upper jaw during talking, eating, or rest. This purity of meeting between similar jaws suggests that even meeting of similar people, such as sex between married cousins, is impure and requires purification. The word "beard" is probably from "be hard," meaning difficult, serious, and strict. In Arabic, the beard is *lehya* derived from *leh haya,* which means it has purity and chastity. Prophet Muhammed (peace be upon him) had a long beard, so it is recommended in Islam that men not shave off their beards.

Women have no facial hair, such as a moustache and beard, as hair to the skin is joining of opposite and has ideas of impurity, and women are supposed to be extra pure creatures. Likewise, men in heaven will have no beard and moustache in Islam suggests purity. Young boys also have no moustache or beard until puberty, since childhood is meant to be a pure time, devoid of sexual ideas or acts.

If men realised how handsome they look with beard they wouldn't shave them. This is because beard is a quick way to differentiate men from women and is therefore a sign of masculinity. Heterosexual women usually find bearded men sexually attractive. The facial hair in males emphasises the sex plan in the face, since hair is without feeling and is touching the skin that has feeling, so it is a meeting of opposites, like sex. This means that traditionally, men were considered to have greater sexual desire to women, however Prophet Muhammed (pbuh) said women have greater sexual desire but it is masked by their shyness and sense of shame. Prophet Muhammed (pbuh) also said the men of heaven will have no facial hair, and this is because facial hair carries sexual meanings, and holy men are pure religious elite. For this reason, Prophet Muhammed (pbuh) commanded men to shave their moustache and grow the beard.

Neck

The neck joins the head, which has the face that has no union between the male nose and female mouth, to the body, where the union of sex happens between male and female genitalia. The neck, therefore, represents need or desire. In Arabic, it is called *ragba,* meaning ambition or hope. People usually beautify the neck with jewellery signify their desire for good things. Men in Europe wear formal clothes, which include a necktie that could mean their sexual desire is under control or limited. Conversely, Arabs of Sudan do a neck dance by bending backwards and rocking their head back and forth, conveying a sense of contentment and prosperity.

Adam's apple which is a hard flesh in men's neck, mean that men have great bodily strength and so can easily achieve their goals and aims.

Chest

Chest, in Arabic, is *sadr*, which means source, as it is the part of the body where there is joining and giving and end of arms and hands that take. It has breasts in women, which are two large round flesh. In Arabic, it is called *thady* derived from *saw ady*, meaning "says given," or *shattor*, meaning smart. As two flesh near the face where the pure union is, it explains the idea of the face, so it is a symbol, or it is being smart.

Breasts are exclusive to females and signify the capacity for nurturing and giving birth. The existence of flesh on a woman's chest is to emphasise the joining of male and female in the face, from which more flesh—meaning a new born—is made. It is different from the breast in animals where their udder is near the genitalia, to emphasise their animal nature and inferiority to humans. The presence of breasts is a prophecy that women give birth to children. This is why men don't have breasts, even though they have nipples.

Breast in English is possibly derived from "be rest," suggesting that once given they provide a sense of rest. Alternatively, "boobs" could stem from "be oops," implying knowledge or intelligence. Breasts symbolise giving and being smart. For this reason, they produce milk, which symbolises knowledge. Water is purity, as it has nothing to be sensed, and white is the colour of purity, so white water is to emphasise its purity. Milk in Arabic is *Laban* derived from *le yabbin,* literally meaning anything that clarifies or informs.

Breasts have nipples called *halma,* which in Arabic is derived from *hilm,* meaning dream or prophecy. The giving of the breast also has a small giving that is nipple or prophecy that giving of sex produces a small child. Nipples are possible from "nay pull less," not giving less, meaning giving more, or extra. In Islam, babies are to be breastfed for two years. Modern science agrees with the benefits of breastfeeding. Men have nipples too, suggesting they contribute in the giving of the baby.

Limbs

Humans have four limbs; two arms, and two legs. Four is the number of awareness since four-sided square corners can be felt and known. This emphasises the idea that the human form knows purity and can therefore know and worship God.

Hands

The hands have five fingers when stretched out. Four fingers are forward in direction, and one small to the side called the thumb. The four fingers represent male since a four-sided joined creates a square in that its corners are felt. Conversely, the absence of corners and the inability to be felt characterise the straight, unjoined finger, which represents the female. In this interpretation, the right hand symbolises the male and female joining in the face, and since it is a permanent union, the right hand is usually strong. The left hand is weak because it symbolises the joining of a male and female in genitalia in sex, and as it is a temporary joining, the left is a weak hand in most people. For this reason, the hand is the support or confirmation of the joining of male and female in the face. Therefore, hands serve as confirmation or affirmation of the union depicted in the face, often utilised in contracts or greetings to express firmness or peace.

In Islam, Muslims join the thumb and middle finger in a circle and raise the index to praise God. This gesture implies the minimisation or absence of the middle. It means purity since the middle is a place of dirty genitalia. Moreover, raising the index finger called *Sababa,* conveys praise for God despite its proximity to the small thumb. Together, these gestures express adoration for God's purity.

People clap by joining the two hands together, which symbolises praise for the union of male and female in genitalia, represented by the left hand in purity and goodness like the purity of the joining of the male and female in the face symbolised by the right hand.

People beautify the fingers and hand with jewellery, such as wedding rings. The ring is round and round represents need since it's a bent line, and rings are usually made of metal such as gold and silver which represents strength and power. Therefore, gold ring suggests the need for security since in marriage all needs of the individual, including sexual desire, are fulfilled. Bracelets worn in the wrist symbolise beauty and acquisition, which reflect the hand's role in acquiring and achieving. The Quran says the people of paradise will be wearing bracelets, and this is to celebrate their riches that they get in heaven.

In Islam, Muslims are commanded to use the left hand in cleaning the genitalia and using the right hand for eating food and in greeting people. which symbolises purity. The Prophet Muhammed (peace be upon him) said the devil eats with his left hand.

Legs

The legs are two, emphasising the number of genders required to create life. Each leg is then divided into two: a thigh and calf by the knees. This further emphasises the need for both genders and shows how vital legs and feet are for walking and long-distance movement. Thus, this design of humans having two legs is a nod to the notions of the purity of the two genders, and their importance in creating new human life. This purity is a sign that humans were created by a pure creator, God.

Legs are the two pillars that help the human stand tall. They are two in number to emphasise purity since two is the number of genders needed for life.

Feet

Legs end in a forward flesh called feet. They help balance humans when standing, which is called *gadam* in Arabic.

Feet also end in small fingers called toes. Feet point forward to mean humans stand on purity and signs of God, since the forward parts of the genitalia (the vagina and penis) are purer than the backwards parts (the anus). Therefore, the feet are in the direction of what is better in the human. Prophet Muhammed (peace be upon him) said paradise lies under the feet of mothers, praising women and being obedient to parents.

As feet mean humans are praiseworthy since they protrude forward, things placed under the feet signify humiliation.

Nails

Nails are the clear hard material at the end of fingers and toes. They expose the flesh underneath as if to say the end (death) comes if the body is cut and internal flesh is exposed. This exposure of flesh in the nail is seen as immodest; therefore, women traditionally covered their nails with henna and nail varnish in modern times. Covering the nails also carry meanings of safety and chastity. It is reported that Prophet Muhammed (peace be upon him) questioned a lady for not having henna covering her nails since it carried meanings of modesty, safety, and chastity.

Shoulder

The shoulders are the end of the arms, and the edge of the upper chest. Hands and chest have the meaning of being given, since the shoulder is in the direction near the face, where there is the permanent union of the male and female in purity. In English, it is probably from the words "sure all they," meaning a lot of giving. In Arabic, the shoulder is *katif*, derived from "*ka ati fi*," meaning giving in it. Interestingly, people usually carry their belonging on their shoulders, such as backpacks.

Sweating

The human skin releases a foul-smelling liquid called sweat. This happens especially after exerting effort such as exercise. It is a clear liquid so it's pure. However, its unpleasant odour may suggest that even purity, such as abstaining from sexual activity, can lead to negative consequences, such as human extinction. Prophet Muhammed (peace be upon him) advised people to cleanse their body at least once every five days.

Movement such as exercise causes sweat, and sweat is a foul smelling liquid, so it means being told that purity is no good. Therefore commanding proximity between male and female in sex. The sweat of Prophet

Muhammed (pbuh) was perfume, as he was a pure man. In fact his smell was so strong in the streets he walked on that people in his time could tell when the Prophet had just passed by.

Belly

Belly in Arabic is *battun* derived from "*bi ati ni*," meaning what comes to it. This is because it is below the chest and above the genitalia. Belly is seen as attractive in women, as it is a reminder of pregnancy and sex.

Prophet Muhammed (pbuh) had no belly; it was on the same level with his chest.

Genitalia

As humans are created by God, a pure being, the area where joining occurs is considered impure. In humans, the middle is a place of exit of excrements such as urine, faeces, and farts, as well as semen in males and menstrual blood in females. All these things are considered impure in Islam and require ritual purification by washing with water before prayer or reading the holy Quran.

Traditionally, women were considered more beautiful and are beautified as it was considered to compensate for lack in genitalia. That lack of penis in women and the vagina being a hole is disappointing to consider, so

God beautified women to make this better as a form of kindness on women. This meant that it is women who make effort to look more beautiful and in Islam men are prohibited from wearing gold jewellery and silk clothing, thus, these beauty items are reserved for women only.

Arabs traditionally saw obsessing about genders as perverted, especially lowering women due to being absent in genitalia. In Arabic, female is *untha* (forgotten), while male is *zkar* (remember), meaning forgotten or remembered to be given flesh in genitalia. Prophet Muhammed (pbuh) said hundreds of thousands of angels curse those who contemplate other people's genitalia. In the Quran, God addresses both genders with masculine as it is considered more formal and proper, except when female believers requested and then God revealed verses using female pronouns.

Arab people wear long clothes that don't emphasise the waist so as not to attract attention to genitalia. This is because Arabs have to survive the desert and be careful of harm, and therefore don't wear clothes that emphasise in the middle as a form of avoiding harm and offence.

Humans cover their genitalia so as not to be offensive by exposing themselves and being reminders of foul and harm. Covering is seen as a symbol of good, kindness, politeness, and a sign of faith in a pure God.

Prophet Muhammed (pbuh) said "modesty is from faith"(Bukhari). It is the case that around the world there are rules against nudity in public.

In all humanity, there is traditionally a head cover to emphasise thoughts of kindness as does covering genitalia. In the west women used to cover face with nets lowered from hats.

Urinating

Humans urinate by excreting yellow water called urine. Yellow, as mentioned before, signifies harm since it lacks the purity associated with white. When water, typically clear, appears yellow, it implies the presence of harm in its absence. In Islam, urinating is considered impure and a person must wash from it before prayer.

Farting

Humans also pass wind, which is called farting. This is excreting foul-smelling air from the anus. Air, as mentioned before, represents need or desire since it requires to be moved before it can be sensed. Therefore, farting can be interpreted as indicating the undesirable nature of sexual desire, as the air stinks. This debasing of sex is pure and therefore human farting is part of the pure design of the human. The term "farting" is possible from the word "far," meaning a lack of union and for male and female to be far from each other. Some farts come with a sound, as if to attract attention to the message it gives. People are embarrassed about farting in public, since no one wants to be told to be pure and chaste; for it assumes they are perverts.

Defecating

Humans defecate by releasing foul-smelling solids from the anus. This is the leftovers from the food that is digested. The fact that the food divided in the mouth by teeth is squeezed by the intestines into a solid emphasises that the genitalia is a place of union of the female and male genitalia during sex. The fact that faeces smell bad suggests joining is bad, or that sex is impure. This means defecating is also a sign of purity in the human. Again, since it carries meaning of sex and is impure, Muslims wash themselves after defecating before they can pray. Faeces are usually brown in colour. Brown, being a shade preceding black, conveys a sense of absence or scarcity, and reflects the remnants left behind after food consumption.

The Quran says that Jesus ate food, meaning Jesus also defecated and can't be God, since the act is not pure enough. Allah, the God of Islam is considered to be whole in purity.

The Genitalia

The female and male genitalia are reactions to harm of excrement in the middle of humans. In the female genitalia, the vagina goes inside from harm, and in the male genitalia, the penis escapes outward overcoming the harm.

Female Genitalia

Females have three holes in their genitalia. The top is the urethra which exits urine; the middle is the vagina, the exit of menstrual blood; and the bottom is the anus, which exists faeces. The middle hole, called the vagina, is also the entrance of the penis during sex and the baby's exit during labour.

Vagina is an empty tube that releases a sticky clear liquid when desiring sex. This lubricant is not only arousing to males but also helps the penis to penetrate the vagina. In Islam, women who release this liquid from a wet dream or orgasm after sexual desire or masturbation must do a wash called *"gusul"* that is usually done after sex, at the end of a period or before pilgrimage.

Black skin genitalia is seen as prettier in women. Black is the colour of absence, and female genitalia is absent flesh. This is why some men are attracted to dark skinned women. This is also the reason why wearing black by women as seen as being sexually provocative and beautiful. The female companions of Prophet Muhammed (pbuh) were sad to find only black fabric when the command to cover came in Islam. However, some literalist (Salafi) scholars have found this an excuse to cover the whole of Arabia's women in black.

In Sudanese Arabic, female genitalia is called *Jamal* which means "what makes beautiful" since women and men's bodies are similar and the only main difference is in the genitalia, so they see this as the main point of attraction.

Clitoris

The clitoris is a small round flesh on top of the vulva and genitalia of females. Clitoris in Arabic is *bazar,* meaning what is given in harm; that is, small giving such as charity to those in harm. That those harmed people give them little to help them. The clitoris signifies that the female genitalia is a place of harm, need, and absence. This idea of giving to harm is thus pure and supports a pure Creator, God.

The clitoris, a small piece of flesh in the female genitalia is in a way a prophecy of birth to infant.

Labia

The Labia in Arabic is *shifareen,* which conveys the concept of spreading or expansion. This terminology suggests that there is no giving in female genitalia. Just as people spread or escape, such as in famine, to a place where they may get food there is spread flesh in female genitalia. This further emphasises the female idea of absence in the female genitalia.

Vertical lips is a vulgar term for the labia minora or majora of the vagina. It also shows that there is a general understanding that the face has sexual association. In Sudan they had a dirty joke that said the larger the man's nose, the greater the size of his penis.

Uterus

The uterus may come from "you it are us," meaning kindness and mercy to others as if they are ourselves. In Arabic, the uterus is *rihim,* meaning mercy. The uterus carries these meanings since it is a round empty muscle in genitalia; round symbolises need, and genitalia is harmful, so the total meaning is the absence of harm, which is mercy. In Islam, women are not required to fight in war, understanding that killing goes against their character of mercy.

Hymen

The hymen may come from "he mean," which in Arabic means *bakara* or *"aba ka ra at,"* meaning not give as seen, akin to illusion. Physically, it refers to flesh destroyed during first sexual intercourse. In its destruction, the women then become serious and mature. The hymen is extreme femininity. It is special since its destruction informs of death. Traditionally, its presence has been associated with cousin marriage, which serves as a reminder to individuals that their physical bodies will be destroyed in death and must be careful while alive.

Menstruation

In girls at puberty, blood exits from the vagina; it is a sign of maturity and a sign that the body is ready to have sex and give birth. Therefore, in Islam, it is the age when marriage is allowed and a person becomes accountable to God. This blood is called period or menstruation. Blood symbolises joining or union, and for it to exist means an emphasis on the absence of female genitalia, indicating a desire for completion or fulfilment, particularly in the context of sexual intercourse. For this reason, it is seen as an embarrassing and impure time.

In Islam, women do not pray the five daily prayers or fast during this period and do not enter the mosque.

This is because God is pure and does not accept impurity. Blood is impure due to its association with union or joining, represented by its red colour. While water typically symbolises clarity and purity, the addition of red transforms its meaning, which signifies joining and impurity. This shift highlights blood's role in conveying the idea of joining and impurity, contrasting with the purity associated with water. Blood in the body is moved in vessels by the pumping action of the heart, which means moving from the meaning of joining and impurity to the meaning of pure joining, as is the plan of humans.

As sexual desire is intense and painful, Prophet Muhammed (peace be upon him) gave an example of consummating the marriage as soon as the male and female reach puberty, citing the intensity and natural inclination of sexual desire. It is controversial in our modern world where government laws give marriage in late teens, around 16, and not necessarily with puberty, as was traditionally seen in humans.

Male Genitalia
Penis

Males have a long flesh away from the harm of the genitalia, and it is called a penis, possibly derived from "pain ease," meaning to escape harm in genitalia, or dick, "they ok." In Arabic, the penis is called *zib*, derived from "*az ab*," meaning to refuse harm as an escape and overcome meanings of harm in genitalia. The penis ends in a smooth sensitive area called the glans.

The penis as the male organ carries ideas of overcoming harm, as well as ideas of safety and comfort. Therefore, it is an idea that females find good and sweet, and is the basis of the female sexual attraction to men. When the penis further hardens and stretches forward–an erection– it is further found more attractive to the females.

Foreskin

The foreskin is the skin that covers the tip of the penis, and its equivalent in females is the clitoral hood. This skin covers the genitalia of the newborn baby as they exit the vagina of the mother, preventing any notions of sex or the joining of the baby genitalia to the mother's genitalia during birth. This means they are a sign of great purity in the human being. In Islam, it is recommended to remove these masses of skin before marriage, so that the person can then join their genitalia with that of their spouse without barrier.

Testicles

Male genitalia have two round balls of flesh called testicles. Round means need, and to be filled with flesh means need to be given. There are two testicles because two is the number of genders and what is required to give life. In Arabic, *khisya* is derived from "*khi si ya it*" (wrong for harm to be given). In English, the word "testicles" is possibly from "taste kill less." They emphasise giving penis flesh, so it suggests giving and feeling no harm. This state of good is purity and goodness and a sign of God.

Semen

Semen is produced in the testicles and comes out of the penis after puberty. In Arabic, it is called *mani*. It is a white sticky liquid. *Mani* means "fulfilling wish." It is white, which signifies purity or goodness, and sticky, meaning joining or union. The semen is white, since white echoes the colour of light, and therefore it is no surprise that semen is responsible for human reproduction. Again, since semen carries meaning of sexual union, its release requires a purification.

When men touch women during sex, and confirm that she is female, weak and a gentle creature by penetration, they ejaculate semen that will fulfil her desire for a baby. Semen comes from "see am men", showing his manliness in being able to fulfil the needs of the woman.

Semen is very arousing to heterosexual women and is sweet to think about. This is because semen which is *mani* from *muna* in Arabic means "wish fulfilled". This way, it was always known as the reason for pregnancy. This is also the reason why the child is usually given their father's name, as it was seen the man willed for the child to be born.

Sex

As mentioned before, the female and male genitalia are reactions to the harm (foul excrements) in the genitalia. The female genitalia go inward from the harm creating the vagina and the male genitalia escape outward from the harm creating the penis. Then when the man sees the female genitalia, he considers the harm as overwhelming from the female reaction to it; therefore, causing an erection. Then the penis wishes to feel the womb since it has ideas of mercy and comfort, so the man penetrates the vagina with his penis. The female enjoys the fact that the absence of the vagina is filled by the flesh of the penis, and this is like a generous giving the poor. The man being strong in body also brings comfort to the woman, making her feel safe and protected. The Prophet Muhammed (peace be upon him) described the orgasm felt in sex, which is an intense pleasure like honey. Females achieve orgasm by vagina muscle contraction and releasing more lubricants that catch the semen and facilitate its entry to the womb for conception and pregnancy.

The Quran commands men to provide for women, and it's a great pleasure for both, since it mirrors the act of sex, where the male gives flesh to the female through the penis penetrating the vagina. Since women are given to, they are aware of this, making them feel shy and embarrassed. This is also the reason some rude and sexist people want to make women feel less and inferior.

Since in traditional heterosexual couples men give to women, homosexual women are called lesbians probably from "less being" since they wouldn't want to take from men, while homosexual males are called gay, meaning happy to get more. In traditional Arab, Muslim society especially, scholars practiced *zuhud* (rejecting riches of this world) by not wanting much as a form of emphasising heterosexuality, purity, and firm belief in an afterlife.

Sex is the joining of the male and female genitalia, and it is only allowed after marriage in Islam. It is the way of creating new humans. Sex is a mirror of the union of the male and female in the face, so sex proves the existence of God. Prophet Muhammed (peace be upon him) said in the act of sex there is *sadaga,* which does not only mean charity, but also truthfulness, since sex gives truth to the existence of God. This is one of the reasons for sex in paradise, and the existence of the celestial virgins (*huor*) in heaven.

Prophet Muhammed (pbuh) is reported to have had sex with all his wives, who were around ten in one night. He had extra sexual strength and said men in heaven will likewise have greater sexual desire and stamina. This is because sex teaches the existence of God and, therefore, was liked by the prophets and men of heaven.

Female genitalia is viewed as being cute and sweet by heterosexual men. Since women can't do much harm due to less bodily strength, men feel comfortable around them— especially when they are virgins—but anxious and careful around other men. In the same way females see babies and young children as being cute and sweet because they are harmless and innocent. The fact that the heterosexual man finds pleasure in women due to them being gentle and kind, made heterosexuality to be traditionally seen as being the best kind of love. Homosexuality, on the other hand, was seen as being without mercy and harsh since there is no love for women and children, and therefore had a strict punishment around the world, usually based on religions.

Because the nose in the face symbolises the penis and it is above the mouth that symbolises the vagina, traditionally people have sex with the man on top of the woman, or what is called the missionary position. The Prophet Muhammed (peace be upon him) is quoted to have said no female has enough from a male and no land has enough from rain and no scholar has enough from knowledge.

In Islam, sex outside marriage (fornication or adultery) is severely punished even in death because such act is seen as playing with life as sex is the means by which new life is created. Playing with life is seen as dangerous and is the path to murder.

Male penis going forward from the level of the skin means it can overcome harm. Since the vagina is inside, this implies that males have twice as much flesh in the genitalia than women, therefore, men inherit twice as much as women in Islam. Since women have no penis and have the empty vagina with no flesh, this mirrors the no joining in the face and the empty space between the nose and mouth, meaning women symbolise God. The Quran has a chapter called women, and Prophet Muhammed (pbuh) said one of the most beautiful things in the world are women.

During first sex, vagina muscles are closed, so that it's difficult penetrating and can be painful or uncomfortable for the girl. This is another sign of purity in humans because it stops male and female genitalia from joining easily. Prophet Muhammed (pbuh) said women in paradise keep returning to virginity state after every sex act.

First sex is special as the hymen is torn and bleeds. This is to know death and that their bodies will also destroy after death just like the hymen is destroyed. This way, they are more careful and vigilant of their safety. When the bride is a virgin her man knows that no other man has touched her or is interested in his wife sexually or wants more of her, and this gives the man peace of mind.

Part of the sexual pleasure for women is when they feel the penis touch the vulva and enter the vagina, and this pleasure is like hero appreciation. That the strong penis that overcomes harm, is interested in the female genitalia that is inwards and escaped inside from the harm of the foulness of the genitalia.

Sex in humanity is considered shameful as it involves the dirty and impure genitalia. For this reason, it was traditionally done by married people only and usually in the middle of the night so as not to be seen. This means that there are laws against public display of affection, nudity and sexual acts in public, and this is very strict especially in Arab and Muslim cultures. In fact traditionally, in Arab and Muslim cultures, people married their cousin as a form of keeping sexual acts hidden. This is because cousins share same blood and flesh, and so there is no telling of them being different and genitalia ideas are hidden. However, strangers getting married have different blood and flesh. This emphasises the difference in genitalia, and meeting during sex just as they are different and become joined in marriage. The Quran says "your wives are a cover for you and you are a cover for them"(2:187) which means that we should marry relatives where the sexual act is hidden, and not strangers where the sexual act is exposed. Arabs also married cousins since this means the children wouldn't know about sex from their parents who are similar in blood and flesh. While children of strangers learn the description of sex from their parents being different and joined in marriage. The Quran commands cousin marriage in chapter of the Groups, verse 50. Arabs such as Sudanese Arabs have the name Alsir (the secret) and in gulf Arabs Maktoom (hidden) as their names, as a way of encouraging and being proud of cousin marriage culture and how it hides sexual descriptions from society.

In a hadith, Eve is said to have said to Adam that it was through sex they got children, because sex is a sign of God the creator, so it was the way to create. What Eve said can also be interpreted as saying "very good, please more" or "more of this" after they had sex. Everyone is created and born from sex, except Jesus born from the Virgin Mary as a miracle of God, Adam and Eve, and more recently, those created from IVF.

Waist:

Women usually have small waists, where flesh goes inwards into body. It is called in Arabic *khisr* (loss). It is considered very beautiful, highlights women's genitalia, that also goes inward so it is very sexually arousing. It is like a prophecy, and an indication that the person is female.

Wide hips are also considered beautiful in women, not only are they practical to aid childbirth, they also hold meanings of loss and femininity, because when things are vertical and on top of each other, they join, but when horizontal no joining occurs. Therefore, the horizontal hips remind and indicate that there is loss in the genitalia, and that there is a hole and emptiness in the vagina.

Buttocks

Buttocks, also known as the bum, are referred to in Arabic as*sulub* or *jabat*. It is the flesh behind the genitalia in the lower back. They symbolise a sense of harm or inferiority in relation to the genitalia. This backward flesh signifies a notion of purity. In some cultures, such as some African and Arab cultures, large butts are seen as beautiful, emphasising the fact that women have multiple meanings associated with harm and absence in genitalia, so they are seen as being very feminine.

Skin

The skin is the cover of the flesh. It can only feel if the object is touching the skin. For this reason, the skin emphasises human design in relation to sexual intercourse and the interaction between male and female genitalia. People cover their skin with clothes not only as a form of protection from the sun or cold, but also in modesty and chastity. In Islam, people are commanded to cover in public, especially women.

Some people have a mole or beauty spot, which is a dark spot on the skin, as if pressing on skin or pointing to a certain part of it. And as the skin is touched during sexual relations, this makes moles significant. Therefore, moles were considered a sign of purity and beauty especially on the face, such as on the cheek. The Mahadi, who is a descendant of Prophet Muhammed (pbuh) and a Muslim saviour who comes at the end of times, is described in the hadith as having a mole on his cheek.

Women remove body hair in order to reduce its sexual meaning and to be soft and smooth. This is because hair is devoid of feeling and can feel the touch of the opposite genitalia during sex. For this reason, hair on the body is impure and women shave their body hair as a form of purity and beauty.

Human skin comes in four main colours: they are white, yellow, brown and black. God in the Quran said He created different skin colours for it to be a sign of the existence of God. This is because human colours carry meanings of purity and so prove the existence of a pure God. White is the colour of light, it is not different from it, it is similar and similarity is a purity. Yellow is the colour that comes after white. Just as white onions changes from white to yellow when fried, yellow is the absence of white. Since white symbolises purity and goodness, yellow means harm or impurity. This means yellow skin carries meanings of purity as it says skin where there is touch and sex is impure. Brown comes before black, and black symbolises absence. Therefore, brown means little giving, such as that of a baby, and also means purity. Black is the colour of absence. For example, when fire burns something it leaves black soot, or when there is no light there is darkness. Black skin means purity since it means absence of touch and sex.

Armpits

Armpits have hair in adult humans, and this is because hair has no feeling whilst skin has a lot of feeling, akin to the meeting of opposite genitalia that results in the creation of life. In Islam, since the meeting of different and opposite elements is considered, Prophet Muhammed (peace be upon him) commanded the removal of armpit hair and pubic hair.

Pubic hair

The meeting of hair and skin is impure; pubic hair also grows after puberty, as it shows a person is ready for the meeting of opposite genitalia in sex and pregnancy. It is recommended to be shaved in Islam.

Illness and Disease

Every part of the human body has a meaning, thus, illness and disease have meanings based on the meaning of the diseased part.

Illness such as a cleft palate, is when a child is born with a cut between nose and mouth, emphasising the purity of the human face. As humans, illness carries meaning associated with purity. Prophet Muhammed (pbuh) said God is close to ill people. He (pbuh) also said "fever is from fire", and fire is pure because it is created by touch and when the fire destroys what touched, it is a sign of purity.

Chapter Two

The Internal Design

Internal Body
Brain

The brain is the organ inside the head, responsible for thinking and awareness. In Arabic, it is called *mukh,* derived from "*am khi,*" signifying a major union, or the essence of awareness. It is a white fatty organ. Fat symbolises self and identity. So white fat of the brain means awareness of pure identity, which is synonymous with God. The Quran says humans were created to worship God. It also means it thinks about what is considered goodness and free from harm to oneself or others.

The Chest
Lungs

The lung is possibly from "longs," meaning desire, since it deals with air—an element synonymous with need and lack of awareness. Air is an element that is hidden and can only be felt if moved, such as the flapping of a hand. Movement is purity; as with movement, things become further and more difficult to join. Therefore, air is pure since it can only be felt if moved. The Arabic word for air is also the same word for desire. The lungs, which take in and remove air, expanding and contracting, are thus also pure. Their function of intake and expulsion of air reinforces the notion of purity through separation.

Heart

The heart in Arabic is *galb*, literally meaning, "what turns," which reflects its role in redirecting blood flow against gravity, upwards towards the brain. Blood is impure and symbolises sex, so it turning upwards is purity. The heart is centre between the lungs and slightly to the left. Its location suggests a diminishing weakening emphasis on union within the bloodstream, further increasing purity. As the heart turns blood upwards, it is opposite in action, so the heart is usually used to symbolise romantic love between the different and opposite genders.

The Abdomen
Liver

The liver in Arabic is *kabd*, derived from "*ka aba da*," suggesting a refusal to join or lack of cohesion, looking like a lump of blood with no connection This state of lack of joining to form complex organs is purity and a sign of God. Arabs consider a family with the term liver to mean possession they want to keep. It is also from *"Ka aba ad,"* (lack of giving) signifying hardship, or "leave err," in English implying a remedy for error or wrongdoing. This idea of improvement and betterment is pure, good, and a sign of God.

Kidneys

The kidneys in English could be from the words "kid in ease," suggesting a sense of irony, as if implying, "must be kidding if they think there is ease." This means hardship, since the two kidneys are distantly placed in the human and there is a challenge for them to join since the kidneys are placed further apart to the sides of the abdomen.

Kidneys in Arabic are *killa*, derived from "*kal a,*" meaning what is difficult to touch since kidneys are placed far apart without contact. Therefore, this distance between similar flesh denotes purity. The kidneys produce urine from blood, a yellow foul-smelling water. Water is pure and signifies the absence of joining, as it lacks sensory components, while yellow means harm. Therefore, the total meaning suggests harm in absence, so Arabs called it *bol,* meaning gains. Therefore, it exits from the middle of the body where there are genitalia and the creation of life, as it means joining and gaining.

Bladder

Bladder in Arabic is *Mathana,* derived from "*um si ana,*" meaning "I am major harm" since it stores yellow urine with harmful meanings. In English, the bladder is possibly derived from the words "be lad are," meaning to be strong to overcome major harm. The idea of major harm is in the meaning of the bladder, which notions of harm into sex and joining, thereby contributing to purity.

Spleen

Spleen in Arabic is *tuhal* derived from "*itu hal,*" meaning "give now" or "giving is nice." Similar to the liver, it is blood-rich but internally clot-ridden, which symbolises extensive giving. This blood and a lot of the clots give the meaning of giving a lot, so it means to give a lot. The idea of giving is pure; just like in mixtures and impurity, there is less giving. Spleen in English is possibly derived from "is be lying," denoting disbelief due to abundant giving.

Pancreas

The pancreas is a leaf-shaped organ between the liver and stomach. It is responsible for sugar control. In Arabic, it is called *miathkla,* derived from "*mu ai si kla,*" meaning "not feel harm that destroys." Pancreas in English is possibly derived from "be in care us," signifying care. It is yellow and long, signifying distant from harm; for this reason, it has connotations of care. This removal of harm is kind and pure. Thus, it is no surprising that it is the idea of being sweet and controlling sugar levels.

Stomach

Stomach in Arabic is "*maeda,*" derived from "*am ea da it,*" meaning "what gives major harm." In English, it could be derived from "is too much" or unbearable harm. This is because the stomach breaks down food to the point of liquid. This destruction of food in digestion is pure since it is the opposite of joining and union.

Intestines

Intestines in Arabic is *musran*, derived from "*musir an*," meaning determined, since it is a long flesh that requires discipline to join things in the distance. In English, it is possibly derived from "In test in, " suggesting a challenge that requires determination. This determination is purity, and joining or reaching does not happen easily.

The appendix is a small portion of extra flesh protruding from the intestine. The intestines, due to their long flesh are considered to carry meanings of determination. Therefore, this extra flesh called the appendix carries some extra form of determination. The total meaning is the addition of a baby, which implies that sexual desire is intense in humans and people become determined in their quest for having sex and children.

Ovaries

The ovaries are where the eggs are, and the equivalent in males are the testicles.

Fat

Fat is the white/yellow oily flesh that surrounds the organs in humans. Fat in Arabic is *shaham*, derived from "*shi ham*", which literally means "what is already washed."

This description arises from fat's lack of frank blood, giving it the appearance of being clean. Thus, the cleanliness of the fat is a purity that supports the purity of humans and the existence of God. Traditionally, fat women were considered beautiful because fat was believed to render them pure, chaste and knowledgeable of God.

Traditionally, slim and bony women were seen as unattractive as their hard bodies reminded one of erections in men. In hadith, Aisha (raa), the cousin and virgin wife of Prophet Muhammed (pbuh) was made to gain weight using dates and cucumbers.

Traditionally, fat in overweight women was considered good for the baby, because fat is softer than bones. Hard bones can hurt the child when hugging or breastfeeding, but fat creates a soft cushion for the baby, meaning more comfort and no pain for the child.

Men usually have larger muscles, giving them a defined hard look, while fat is soft and feminine.

While fat was traditionally seen as beautiful, a woman with a smaller body than most men is a modern standard of beauty.

Bone

Bones are the white hard flesh in humans. Bones are very strong, and form the skeleton of the human body. The fact that the bones are white in colour signifies purity, since white is a symbol of purity.

Muscle

The muscles are red flesh that connect bones together. Muscles change shape to contract bones together and are the source of movement in the body. The fact that muscles can create movement is considered pure, since it contrasts with the concept of joining which is deemed impure.

Chapter Three

The Diversity of Human Races

God made humans in six different racial groups: Caucasians, Persians, Asians, Africans, Arabs, and Indians. Then each race is further divided into tribes. In the Quran, God says He created humans in races and tribes so that they may come to know each other in peace.

The races not only differ in skin colour; each race also emphasises a different aspect of human life. The African race emphasises the idea that humans need to maintain life by eating or defending themselves from predators. The Arab race represents the idea that humans have a mind and can think and make decisions. The Indian race represents rest and comfort. The Caucasian race represents the idea that humans create and make things. The Persian race signifies order and humans can therefore predictability, suggesting that humans possess the ability to organise and anticipate events, such as remembering the location of objects. The Asians represent restoration, improvement.

God created humans in races to show the deliberate design of creation by a higher power. Just as a new mother proudly showcases her newborn, the existence of racial groups highlights the attention and care bestowed upon humanity by God.

God gave the different races a suitable land or continent. For instance, since Africans are people of life and maintaining the body, their land is filled with many animals. Arabs, who are known as thinkers, live in a harsh desert that needs them to be mindful. Caucasians live in cold regions so as not to overheat from creating and hard work.

God also gave each race a look that suits their race's agenda. For instance, Africans are black and this covers their inner flesh so that their veins don't show. It is also a reminder not to get injured or expose flesh as it leads to death. Africans short coarse hair suggests death is not good, as hair lacks sensation akin to a lifeless body. Caucasians are white and their white skin is reminiscent of the colour of light, and creating sometimes involves repeating things. Since Arabs are people of the mind, and must be careful in the desert. God sent Prophet Muhammed (peace be upon him), who is the greatest Prophet ever and was an Arab, to warn people of God's hellfire and to be careful of it by worshiping God.

To end racism means to understand humanity and the different races, what they look like, their languages and culture, and respecting them. Historically, no one who understood the races ever doubted the humanity of a different race and wanted to destroy them. A royal must contact other tribes and races and make contact with those of authority among them to negotiate peace, trade, and exchange knowledge. They also spread knowledge about different tribes and races for a better understanding and acceptance of humanity.

The African Race

The African race represents life and its needs such as eating and protecting the body from injury and damage. They are majorly dark-skinned to cover flesh and veins as a reminder not to get injured and expose the flesh, since it leads to death. This emphasis on the body in the African race means their land is full of bodies of creatures. Their hair is short and coarse, even in females. This signifies that death is bad, since hair is lifeless and without feelings, like a dead body. Their facial features are usually large and with irregular outline; this suggests Africans are people of truth and trust. Since the human face shares similarity in design with the genitalia and sex, it is therefore not right for it to be considered good, as a way of being truthful. The Prophet Muhammed (peace be upon him) in one Hadith said Africa is a land of truth. Truth is important to life, for fake food doesn't nourish life, but real food does, so truth is essential to life.

As Africans are proud of their bodies and strength in seeking life, they were proud of their bodies and so they traditionally lived naked. They also cut the lips and stretched them using discs as a form of emphasising eating and its support of life. They also loved wearing beads, since beads are round symbolising desire, and they used wearing many beads as a form of expressing great desire for life.

In North Africa, tribes such as Coptic and Berber are white-skinned and black-haired. It signifies a look of beauty and emphasises that the body is special to Africans. There are also Nubian Africans who some are brown skinned and live as natives in North Sudan and South

Egypt. Since Africans give importance to life and food, these things are a must (slave to life), thus the association of slavery with Africans even though there were slaves in all races. The idea of "Black Lives Matter" is not only beautiful for seeking justice against discrimination but it is literally true, African people find life as being very important. In Arabic, Africans are called Sudan and Habasha. There was a famous African companion of Prophet Muhammed (peace be upon him) called Bilal who made the call to prayer. In early Islam, Prophet Muhammed (peace be upon him) sent his companions and family to Africa, fearing prosecution of the Arabs of Mecca.

The Arab Race

Arabs represent the mind and thinking faculty in humans. They live in the harsh dangerous desert, and so must be responsible, make good choices, and think carefully so as not to be harmed. As Arabs must think about survival, the greatest expression of this is by giving birth so as to be survived by a child after death. Arabs understand sex to be best between married cousins since cousins are related and so there is no suggestion to the genitalia which are different in men and female and places where dirt exits. Also, cousin marriage emphasises the existence of a pure

God since they are creating new life by their union, which is pure.

God chose to have His house built in Arabia, in the middle west of Arabia, as it symbolises purity. Since genitalia is in the middle and west is where the sun sets, it means covered, an absence of genitalia or an absence of sex.

God uses the term "Arab" in the Quran to describe women of heaven, because they understand and desire sex like the Arabs.

Many Arabs especially those in the gulf area are light skinned and black haired, meaning the meeting of the opposite colours. This alludes to the concept of reproduction with the ultimate aim of continuing the lineage through the survival of offspring. However, there are brown skinned Arabs who modernly live in Sudan, whose look doesn't emphasise sex, as sex has ideas of harm and Arabs are against harm and danger. Brown Arabs are usually from Hejaz region of Arabia, a safe place where the house of God is. Also, Hijaz is western Arabia where the sun sets, signifying the lack of light and sun, making it most suitable for the brown Arabs who are dark. The colour brown is lighter than black—the colour of absence. Brown was considered to mean little giving, and since being Arab is related to having children, which is giving or getting a little baby, brown was considered to be a colour most suitable for Arabs. There are also black-skinned Arabs, and this is because black is the colour of absence, and for skin to be black means absence of touch or sex, so it represents extra safety since sex involves the genitalia where there is dirt and harm.

There are Arabs with coarse hair. This is because hair cannot feel, and since Arabs have children, their coarse hair suggests it is not good to be devoid of feeling, touch and sex. Coarse hair also means purity since the hair meeting the skin is meeting of opposites and is impure so the coarseness of the hair signifies impurity is not good.

Prophet Muhammed (peace be upon him) said love of the Arab is a sign of belief in God. This is because belief in God is about safety from hellfire and Arabs are people who care about safety in the desert. So, to love Arabs is to appreciate safety. Arabs like gold, perfume and all things beautiful and nice, since they are the opposite of harm and danger.

The Persian Race

Persians are a race representing order, prediction, and prophecy in humans. As humans, we can retrieve our clothes in the cupboard, predicting they are there after we place them. The Jews who descended from Abraham from Iraq are most likely a tribe from the Persian race, and therefore there have been many prophets and prophecy in their people. The Persians are light-skinned with black hair, which is the meeting of opposites and a prediction of the existence of the opposite gender.

The Prophet Muhammed (peace be upon him) spoke about how keen the Persians are about religion. Salman was a Persian companion of Prophet Muhammed (peace be upon him) who made an arduous journey, seeking one priest after another, and seeking the true religion. Jerusalem is a city in far western Persian land so it means the end of prophecy, or a dream coming true. Therefore, it is considered holy in Islam.

The Indian Race

Indians are a race representing rest and leisure in humans. Their land has so much spice as spice relaxes and rejuvenates the senses just like rest. They have a great art scene in Bollywood movies that are famous around the world. These movies are great for relaxation and part of the expression of their race. Arabs named their daughter Hind, which is the Arabic word for India, meaning they should rest and be comfortable. A famous Hind, is a companion of Prophet Muhammed (peace be upon him) who took revenge on the Prophet's uncle, Hamza, by chewing his liver after assassinating him.

The Caucasian Race

Caucasians are a race representing innovation and makings things by humans. Their land is cold, protecting them from overheating from the effort of creating. They are light-skinned, as white is the colour that repeats light. The Quran has a whole chapter called "Romans," which is the Arabic word for Caucasians. God designates these racial characteristics as signs of divine creation, as they are often depicted as signs of creativity and purity due to their white skin. Caucasians love doing things as hobbies, such as crafts and DIY. From a young age, children in Caucasian countries are taught to make and create things such as cards and other articles.

The Asian Race

Asians are a race representing human repair, improvement and restoration. As Asians are about fixing, it suits them for their lands to be the East, since it's where God lessens harm of sun by moving it in the sky. Chinese have a history of writing, and marital arts. They are light-skinned with black hair, but some of them, such as native Americans (who are probably part of Asian race), have darker skin. The Chinese are mentioned in the Hadith. Prophet Muhammed (peace be upon him) advised us to seek knowledge even as far as traveling to China.

As humans are made up of races, each human can relate to all the races by finding elements of connection and familiarity across different racial identities. For example, an Arab man in the desert wakes up in the morning to eat food like Africans, fixes tent like an Asian, predicts his clothes in cupboard and fetches them like a Persian, and then takes his camel to an oasis, which is doing something like a Caucasian. Finally, upon his return, he seeks rest and relaxation like an Indian.

As humans are made up of races, each race should emphasise their importance in the world. Africans, for example, should inspire to have a right to free food for the poor. Arabs should advocate for the right to marry their cousin and prioritise education. Indians should advocate the right for breaks and rest in work, and the right to be restored to health like an Asian when ill. There should be a human right to learn about religion and prophecy like Persians and a right to have a job to create like Caucasians.

About the Author

Mysa Elsheikh is a Muslim Arab Queen (Um-fugara or Mother of the Poor) from Sudan. Her full name is Mysa, daughter of Mohamed Elgasim, son of Elsheikh Almagzoub. Mysa traces her lineage directly to Prophet Muhammad (peace be upon him) through both her father and mother. She is also a descendant of Abdullah ibn Abass (raa), Prophet Muhammed's cousin and great Quran scholar. Mysa learned Arabic and the Quran in Sudan as a child, and she attended her grandfather's Quran School (khalwa) with her brother. She once qualified for a high IQ society when she was young, and excelled in subjects like Maths, Arabic, and Religious Education. Her academic journey led her to study Medicine at St George's University of London, where she graduated early with a diploma in Medical Studies. She left Medicine mainly because she wanted to finish her book, *Ihsan*, and pursue a career in writing Islamic books and calling people to God and Islam. She studied a medical summer course at Magdalen College University of Oxford. She also completed a year of Psychology and Creative Writing at Bolton University, in addition to pursuing two years of Medicine at Ahfad University for Women in Sudan.

Inspired by a dream of Prophet Muhammed (peace be upon him) during the Christmas holiday of 2003, she was guided to study Sufism (Ihsan) with her paternal uncle, King Sheikh Jaily, son of Elsheikh Almagzoub of Albaneya, Sudan. In the summer of 2004, she took a formal pact and became initiated into the Sammaniya Sufi Path. Four months later, at the age of 19 years old, Mysa had a vision of God while walking down Longmead Road, in south London, Britain. In the Vision,, Mysa saw God, Allah, the God of Islam. She reports seeing an ocean of light that enveloped her from all directions. The light penetrated everything hard and solid, and it was as if she was drowning in an ocean of light. Before the vision, Mysa had been begging God to give her His vision for months, and this was out of her great love for God and in seeking the divine beauty of God.

Mysa comes from a family of Sufi (Ihsan) scholars, and her grandfathers and forefathers called Magazeeb of Damer were all Sufi scholars and Saints in Sudan for more than 500 years. Mysa was the favourite granddaughter of the great Sufi saint, King Sheikh Magzoub of Albaneya, Sudan (died 1986). In May 2022, she married her first cousin to fulfil verse 33:50 of the Quran, guided by yet another dream of Prophet Muhammed (peace be upon him). In November 2022, she accepted her first Ihsan (Sufi) student. Mysa is a famous influencer in Sudan and as of August 2024, she has over 66,000 followers on TikTok alone and many viral videos watched by millions.

Mysa's Genealogy to Prophet Muhammed (pbuh)

Mysa, daughter of Sharif Muhammed Algasim, son of Sharif Magzoub, son of Sharifiya Sakeena, daughter of Sharif Fadul is the son of Sharif Hussain, son of Sharif Ibrahim, son of Sharif Muhammed, son of Sharif Hamad, son of Sharif Muahmmed Zumrawi, son of Sharif Muhammed Ahmed Al Bagir, son of Sharif Mahmoud, son of Sharif Hamad, son of Sharif Abdalkareem, son of Sharif Hassaballah Abu Khuf, son of Sharif Muhammed Almadani, son of Sharif Jabal, son of Sharif Abdullah, son of Sharif Barakat, son of Sharif Gasim, son of Sharif Rattib, son of Sharif Shahwan, son of Sharif Messaya, son of Sharif Taglab, son of Sharif Hober, son of Sharif Zakir, son of Sharif Sirajaldeen, son of Sharif Ja Alnaser, son of Sharif Gais, son of Sharif Shafi, son of Sharif Fayed, son of Sharif Umayra, son of Sharif Umran, son of Sharif Ali Noraldeen Ameel Murij, son of Sharif Hussain, son of Sharif Hassan Alakbar, son of Sharif Ali Albadri, son of Sharif Ibrahim, son of Sharif Muhammed, son of Sharif Abi Baker, son of Sharif Ismael, son of Sharif Umar, son of Sharif Ali, son of Sharif Usman, son of Sharif Hassan, son of Sharif Muhammed, son of Sharif Mosa, son of Sharif Yahya, son of Sharif Essa, son of Sharif Ali, son of Imam Muhammed Altagi, son of Imam Hassan Alaskari, son of Imam Muhammed Alhadi, son of Imam Muhammed Aljawad, son of Imam Ali Alrida, son of Imam Mosa Alkazim, son of Imam Jafer Alsadig, son of Imam Muhammed Albagir, son of Imam Ali zain Alabdeen, son of Imam Hussain, son of Imam Ali and son of Fatimah, daughter of Muhammed (peace be upon him), the Prophet of Islam.

www.ingramcontent.com/pod-product-compliance
Lightning Source LLC
Chambersburg PA
CBHW070322120526
44590CB00017B/2786